Copyright © 2023 by Madi Swegle

All rights reserved.

No part of this publication may be reproduced, distributed, or transmitted in any form or by any means, including photocopying, recording, or other electronic or mechanical methods, without the prior written permission of the publisher, except as permitted by U.S. copyright law. For permission requests, contact: sweglestory@gmail.com

The story, all names, characters, and incidents portrayed in this production are fictitious. No identification with actual persons (living or deceased), places, buildings, and products is intended or should be inferred.

Book Cover and Illustrations by Moraslana

*Dedicated to the wonderful doctors, nurses, and staff at Mid-Iowa Fertility who made all of our dreams come true.*

*Families are created in so many special and unique ways. In reading this book, I hope that you are able to share your IVF journey with your children in a fun and meaningful way.*

*Every IVF journey is different. If the verbiage in this book doesn't exactly align with your journey or family dynamics, I hope that with just a few select word changes you will be able to accurately represent your personal story.*

*Your family is special and deserves to be celebrated!*

# MORE THAN ALL THE STARS
*an IVF STORY*

YOU KNOW HOW MUCH WE LOVE YOU!
YOU'RE SPECIAL, BRAVE, AND STRONG.
BUT DO YOU EVER WONDER
HOW YOU CAME ALONG?

WE DREAMED OF YOU

AND WISHED FOR YOU

ON MORE THAN ALL THE STARS.

WE HAD TO

WAIT...

AND WAIT...

AND WAIT...

IT WAS REALLY HARD!

WE DREAMED OF YOUR SMILE, YOUR EYES, AND YOUR LAUGH

WE WANTED TO MEET YOU SOON!

WE FOUND A DOCTOR WHO SAID HE COULD HELP

HE SAID: "COME SEE ME THIS AFTERNOON!"!

WE WENT AND MET WITH THE DOCTOR
AND LOTS OF NURSES, TOO
WHO GAVE US PILLS AND DRINKS AND SHOTS
TO HELP US GET TO YOU!

THE DOCTOR HAD A BIG LABORATORY
WITH BEAKERS, MICROSCOPES, AND PIPETTES.
HE TOOK SOME CELLS FROM MOM AND DAD
FOR A PROCESS CALLED IVF.

HE PUT THE CELLS TOGETHER
TO CREATE YOUR EMBRYO.
YOU STARTED OUT EXTREMELY TINY
BUT YOU BEGAN TO GROW AND GROW!

We got updates on you every day,
Our love for you was strong.
We were so excited to meet you,
We hoped it wouldn't be long!

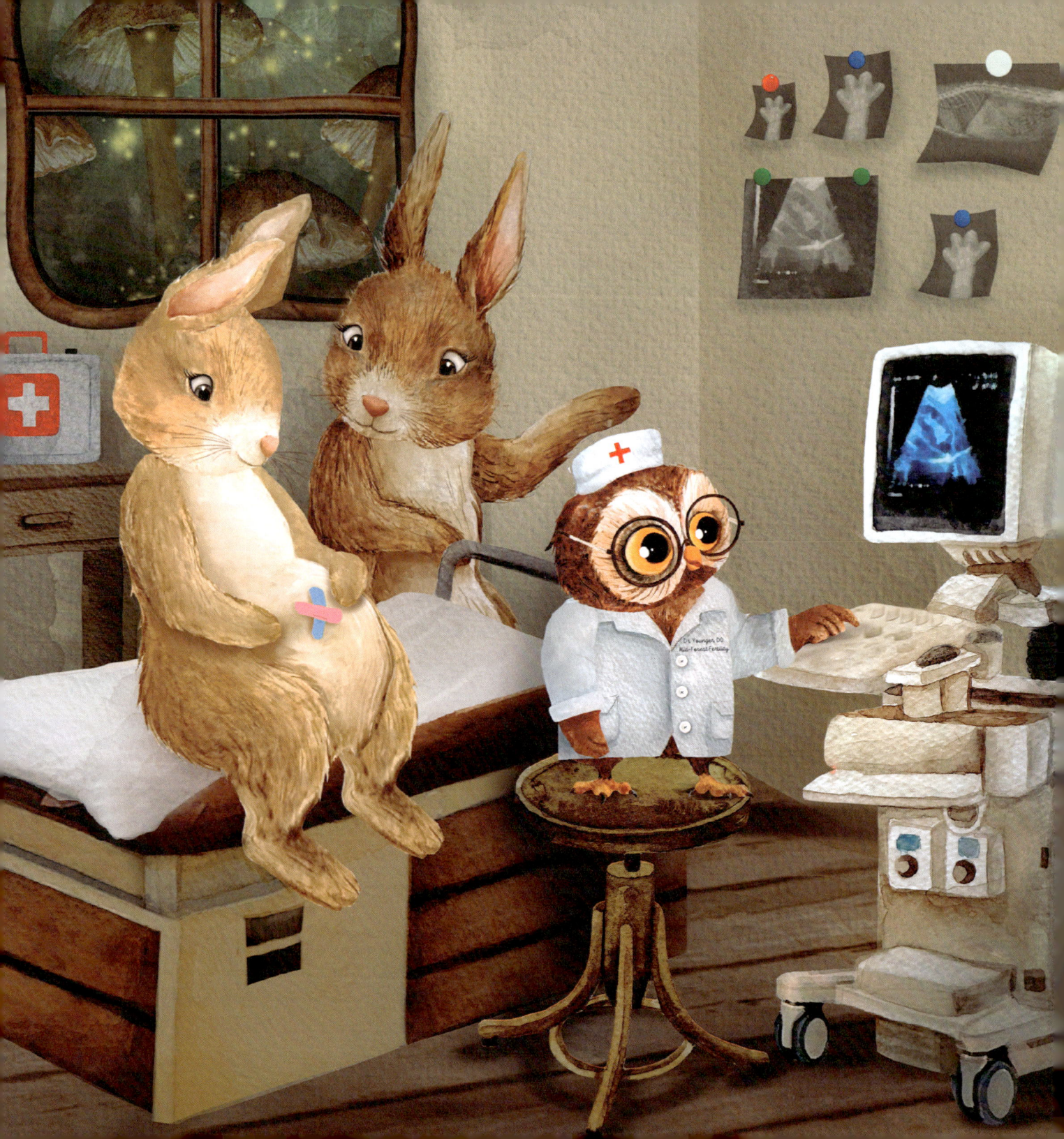

ONE DAY THE DOCTOR CALLED US UP
AND SAID, "THE TIME IS HERE!"
WE JUMPED FOR JOY AND HUGGED AND CRIED
BUT ONLY HAPPY TEARS.

THE DOCTOR GENTLY PUT YOU IN MOM'S TUMMY,
SAFE AND COZY WARM.
THERE YOU HAD THE VERY BEST PLACE
TO BECOME STRONG AND FORM.

YOU GREW IN MOM'S TUMMY FOR MONTHS AND MONTHS!

WE SANG, WE DANCED, WE LAUGHED.

WE PREPARED A ROOM THAT WAS JUST FOR YOU,

EVERYTHING WAS HAPPENING SO FAST!

WHEN YOUR BIRTHDAY CAME AROUND
WE WENT TO THE HOSPITAL.
IT WAS FINALLY TIME TO MEET YOU!
YOU WERE SO CUTE AND SMALL!

AS WE HELD YOU IN OUR ARMS
OUR FACES LIT UP WITH GLEE!
YOUR TINY NOSE AND LIPS AND EYES
WERE MORE PERFECT THAN WE COULD HAVE EVER DREAMED.

WE WISHED FOR YOU

AND DREAMED OF YOU,

NOW YOU'RE IN OUR ARMS.

WE LOVE YOU TO THE MOON AND BACK

AND MORE THAN ALL THE STARS.

www.ingramcontent.com/pod-product-compliance
Lightning Source LLC
Chambersburg PA
CBRC091203010526
44107CB00021B/1236